Those Moments We Fall

By

Darin T. Steele

authorHOUSE™

1663 LIBERTY DRIVE, SUITE 200
BLOOMINGTON, INDIANA 47403
(800) 839-8640
WWW.AUTHORHOUSE.COM

© 2004 Darin T. Steele.
All Rights Reserved.

First published by AuthorHouse 10/20/04

ISBN: 1-4184-7636-6 (e)
ISBN: 1-4184-7635-8 (sc)

Printed in the United States of America
Bloomington, Indiana

This book is printed on acid-free paper.

Acknowledgments

I Darin T. Steele would like to acknowledge all the important people that have helped me along the way. Life is so strange it seems that full circle we fall. At this time, I would like to give special thanks to my mother Mary West; she is my strength and my support system. I love her dearly with all my heart. Also, to my dear friend Ladonna Kearney for all her assistance. She really inspires me. Her poetry is sensational; she is an upcoming author look for her work soon. I thank God for blessing me with the gift because without him I am lost.

-Darin Steele

Durham,N.C.

September 2004

Preface

Please understand clearly that the statements within the contents of this book do not apply to all women or all men. Try to make your own analysis; It's what you perceive as the truth. Many of the statements in this book may or may not be factual. However, let the journey begin; feel the struggle that some people experience in relationships. Embrace the pain that people endure.

Table of Contents

Chapter 1

Relationships

-Sometimes in a relationship

We must stand tall and silent

Like the great wall of Berlin

When two people are lost in love

No one can win

However what appears to be real

Can be fake

A relationship should be based

On give and take

Not on how well

Someone can make or bake a cake

Many nights you may lie and weep

And without true love

You will cry yourself to sleep

But always pray to the Lord for your soul

To keep...

To have someone to hold, is a beautiful thing. The pain in a relationship is the hurt that love sometimes feels. Love is the quest that transcends the test of time. Let your heart and soul travel the path of enlightenment and insightfulness. By chance, the 3d's divorce, desertion, and death devour your potential of having long-term relationships. They take the possibilities of achieving happiness to another level. For, life itself is a calculated risk, and you never know what the future holds. The first of the 3d's is divorce. During this process I can imagine, that someone's hopes and dreams and all they have invested in their relationship seems to have been all for nothing. Sometimes things do not work out as planned; in a relationship one would hope for longevity and prosperity. Maybe, people get married for the wrong reasons. Marriage is a sacred bond that husband and wife share. The values of marriage are somewhat vague because the vows are short lived. Unfortunately, today, in America the overall divorce rate is 1 million strong and counting. With the divorce rate increasing annually, this sets a dangerous precedent for the youth in society. Some marriages have alternative plans; the doubts and fears play a major part. Reality sets in and one realizes that maybe nothing is forever, and things don't always work out. So, instead of having a life long mate, somehow, with luck of the draw people try to remain friends.

The second of the 3d's is desertion. During this process one of the parties in the relationship just leaves, for one reason or another. The deserter leaves with no regard to the loved one's hurt by his or her actions. This person is very selfish, lacking concern for the other person involved. However, the deserter feels that his loved one may be better off without him or her. The deserter often times is a parent. Sometimes parents don't realize the impact they have on their children; they are the biggest influence in their children's lives. Children depend on their parents for guidance and direction. For, charity starts at home; this statement holds truth. Both parents are much needed in the household. Understandably, they play very important roles.

In some cases the deserter has a chance to make a wrong decision right, to become a part of the loved one's life and bridge the gap, so to speak. In the best instance, the deserter can be given a second chance. This can be a very emotional and difficult time for the person most effected by this action. The quickest way to mend the damage that has already been done is not to reflect on the past. The solution of starting from today and taking it one day at a time seems to be efficacious. Finally, the last of the 3d's is death the inevitable, as we look forward to the years ahead death will come to take refuge. Surprisingly, people will begin to die in enormous numbers. This is only the beginning; random and senseless acts of death will become an epidemic. This is only a sign of the time; nothing is new under the sun. The laws of nature will always live out their course. One thing is for certain, people will live and people will die. In the process of life, somehow death has become somewhat of a pyrrhic victory. The losses need to be observed more seriously; the deaths are outcries of no projective gain. We have failed to educate and protect one another and inadvertently risk has become the norm. One should live his or her life to the fullest and die with dignity, which is a peaceful way to die.

Effective communication is very essential in a relationship. In fact, it's the principle source that links or bonds people to one another. It's a vital source, but if not used properly, this source is quite useless. However, when people use communication as an effective tool in their relationship, the capabilities are unlimited, but what confuses this source is people fail to communicate effectively. Therefore, communication is only effective when it's continuous and helps aid in achieving a common goal, also when it completes a task successfully. Relationships have become very difficult and somewhat complex. We live in a world where everything is touch and go. Today's relationships are calling for many people to be the other person. Instead of one lover, some people have the best of both worlds. However, true love is a journey, an odyssey of feelings and emotions that shouldn't travel this endless path of pain. Consequently, people try to hold on to something or someone that may not be right for them. When this happens sometimes your family will turn on you, just for their own self-gratification. Materialistic possessions will become a false sense of comfort for people that endure this kind of pain. This materialistic comfort is their only means of feeling happy because internal sadness and pain have found a permanent and profound place in their lives. Never give yourself to people who do not love you because internally this will kill you a 1000 times over! Relationships can become a struggle for individuality, but don't rely on your partner to give you an identity. Both persons in the relationship must be able to carry one another in times of weakness.

At the beginning, some relationships are made of the power of love. Somehow, the relationship itself causes a malicious digression and love transforms into hatred. The relationship can be bittersweet because the feelings of love are tainted . Many people fall in love, but it seems as if their objective is to fall out of love. Maybe, people that are in relationships have an everlasting internal battle of mixed emotions. I can't soothe the ache of people in relationships having thoughts of loving someone else. Consequently, I believe that simple and seemingly harmless curiosity can become more intense and less controlled if the curious person has constant thoughts about another, other than his or her partner. This is a catalyst that can decrease the love for the current partner and transform compassion into deceit. I feel that if curiosity is present in a relationship then it's safe to say that "While the cat's away, the mice will play."

In a healthy and loving relationship, mutual respect and consideration is present; each person has respect for the other and takes his or her feelings into consideration, and these two components are essential. If respect and consideration are lacking and your partner criticizes and insults you, maybe there's resentment in some form. For instance, if your partner doesn't like the way you perform simple tasks in your daily life, this type of behavior is puzzling; it implies that your partner doesn't allow total acceptance of you as an individual.

There are many issues that need to be addressed in marriages and in relationships. Many people are in marriages where they are hated rather than loved. It's unbelievable that someone could show you eyes of concern and show you hate with those very same eyes. The fact of the matter is, it's an unfortunate way of life for some people. Some marriages endure storms of sorrow and will experience private affairs. Where does trust lie in the midst of deceit; does trust matter in a marriage? To illustrate, "a thin line between love and hate," isn't just a cliche`. Specifically, life is unpredictable and it seems that we are all here to live a life of pain. Most importantly, trust should always matter, and when someone doesn't love you, trust has no merit.

Some people have lost the ability to show and give unconditional love. So many marriages function on a day to day basis with no hope for a real and secure future. Together, doesn't always mean that people are joined for life; maybe it means just for the time being, with no promise of forever and no promise of true love. Marriage has a 50/50 chance of surviving. One can no longer count on sharing life with the hope to always stay happily married. Nevertheless, if married life becomes a bit repetitive, couples should find the fire that keeps the flames burning, like the rising temperature of fresh wood. On the other hand, many people have come to grips with their fears about love and marriage. My hope for the future is that people find real love and live their life with an enriched direction. Although, people will always hurt and heal themselves, since we are subject to struggle.

The fear of not knowing what the future holds in a problematic relationship, could make one lean on the shoulders of others. But the need to still continue the current relationship by trying to force it to work, only magnifies the problem. This is where the cancer begins; a battle for understanding takes place between both partners. Principally, one partner may feel as if he or she is doing what it takes to resolve the problematic relationship. These efforts aren't enough because the relationship has endured emotional scars which will override the efforts put forth. Furthermore, a relationship of this caliber is all but over, and the essence of time is the start of detraction. This relationship isn't healthy for either individual, and there is more pain certain to come. The best solution is to have closure before totally ending the relationship. Closure will enable both people to grasp a firm understanding of their differences, without either having to carry blame, or fault. Clearly, it really doesn't matter by this point, who is right and who is wrong; both parties will move along and find their own way. Having ended the relationship, it will take time for each of them to heal. Consequently, at low points both persons may feel as if they will die, because love is so fierce and unpredictable that it has the ability to pierce your heart at any given moment.

A relationship is a beautiful rose, and it requires nurturing, even as a seed in the ground. Therefore, it must have the same continuous nurturing to keep the flower beautiful. As the relationship blossoms, love is shared that enhances the beauty of the rose. When the foundation of love is almost gone, people must refine its value. Both partners should make the relationship last by loving one another unconditionally. Nevertheless, some people seem to want what is forbidden to them and extra marital affairs have become a way of life in today's society. Many people are searching for some sense of direction. But, for a relationship to endure the test of time each party should play a very important role in the relationship. Also, in a relationship the merit of trust must be safeguarded for eternity. Principal guidelines of any relationship should live for the loyalty of trust. If trust is therefore tarnished in any way, the relationship is somewhat damaged.

However, if psychological and emotional damage has already taken place in the relationship, one must never lose his or her integrity; for, your integrity is what makes one complete. Consequently, some people will experience relationships that consist of malicious intent. The key is to hold on to your integrity and never let anyone change this characteristic about you. Sometimes life brings changes for the worst but don't ever sell your soul for love; stay grounded. Your integrity is a part of your spirit. It is the makings of your soul. To sell your soul for the hopes of love is a painful death that lingers internally. Nonetheless, today's relationships should reveal more favorable characteristics, with men and women working together in their relationships. Men should give women the utmost respect and consideration. Furthermore, women will make better decisions than men will in meaningful relationships.

Some men can't deal with this kind of relationship. Most women want a man that will be understanding and just listen to them. If a man can effectively use this listening strategy, then the chances of conflict decrease tremendously. This can be used as an important preventive measure which will keep the relationship less problematic. Thusly, enabling the relationship to function on a productive and positive level. Nonetheless, the woman still plays a vital part in the relationship and her decision making must be established with trust. If the woman's trust isn't established, the relationship has the potential to become hostile. Respectfully, men should accept more responsibility in the relationship, especially, if there are children involved. Furthermore, in relationships with a family structure, the man should provide for his family, although, the parties may have gone their separate ways.

Some marriages go through legal battles to obtain materialistic possessions and financial gains. However, there should be no need for such legal battles. A real man will let his wife have just about everything, because a real man walks away with the satisfaction of knowing that he's still providing for his family. Also, today's relationships lean more towards the materialistic side of change or discomfort. In, these relationships, some people expect their partner to buy love. But, love and fellowship for one another shouldn't carry a price or markup. Principally, we may feel loved but some people really do not know what love truly is. For, love has to come from the heart; it doesn't have a materialistic price tag. Many people still believe that someone with this type of demeanor could somehow passionately love them; no one should base his or her life around false love and selfishness. Most of the time what is morally wrong about someone will surface in a relationship.

However, the longer someone stays in a relationship of this magnitude, the more he or she is victimized. This person will gradually lose respect for himself, because a relationship must be based on love and trust, and nothing else, but this. Believe it or not, true love is so powerful, that one night without communicating with your partner is too much for the heart to bare. Sometimes, to obtain the truth from some people, is almost like pulling teeth. Often times, the truth will become a flat out lie. It's a special thing to receive the truth, no matter what the circumstances may be. Clearly, stating the truth is hard to come by, therefore, people will lie. Many people will lie to the very end and if given another opportunity to redeem themselves, they will lie again. Surprisingly, the truth can be achieved in a relationship, but what is the likelihood of consistency. To receive the truth on a consistent basis is unbelievable, since the truth to some degree will be fabricated. Therefore, it's perfectly alright to believe in yourself and always follow your instincts and your intuition. Because no one should be lied to under any circumstances; this is the honor that the truth holds.

God could ask for our soul whenever he seeks to. The power of love for one another is our means of security. People cry and grieve at the moment of pain or death, but no one cries with joy for the living. We must open our eyes and feel the pain that our hearts place upon each other daily. People treat one another worse than the devil treats his own servants. Many people feel that they have the right to treat someone else badly. They also expect people to understand their faults and mistakes. Nevertheless, if some people are confronted constructively on an issue their partners may have concerns about, this discussion may cause them to experience tension or stress. Quietly, some people will begin to distance themselves from their partners. They'd do this because they sincerely believe that their partner is wrong for elaborating on certain issues. However, anything that prohibits their relationship from functioning properly, should be questioned or discussed by the parties involved.

Today's society consists of women who are seemingly taking full advantage of their attributes. Today's woman is more confident and self-assured. Also, women seem to have men running in circles and we are victimized by their dance. Consequently, women think faster than men do and they are also far more clever by nature. Some women simply create an atmosphere where everything is dramatized. Indeed, they know men will rhythmically step to the same dance or request. Many women use cognitive thinking as a resourceful tool in communicating the persona or message they want to put forth. A woman's happiness dictates the level of success in the relationship. Specifically, in relationships feelings should be mutual. however, some men are in relationships where they are unhappy, due to the lack of acknowledgment from their partners. Most men will not reveal their true feelings and they just continually endure this not so perfect partnership. They maintain peace in the relationship for the sake of unmerciful love.

In the eyes of some women, men will always have to prove themselves. Somehow, a man never quite accomplishes the task of total acceptance by his woman. Even if the man does totally right by his woman , there will always be something that she dislikes rather than likes. This is why many people say "A man's job is never done;" this statement is true. Maybe this is one of the reasons that causes relationships to be very difficult. The complexity of a woman is like an abstract painting with sheer beauty. This is just the nature of women in today's society. Nonetheless, men in today's relationships are still misunderstanding many women. The standards of some men must elevate; such that they'll become more valued commodities, and contain good, moral qualities and principals. Consequently, some people will have incompatibilities whenever forming relationships. Ultimately, there will always be differences in relationships but at some point we shall find common ground. It's very unlikely that 2 people will agree wholeheartedly on the same thing, 100 percent of the time.

Sometimes in relationships, it doesn't matter what you do to satisfy your mate; it can still seem as though it was all done for nothing. Short-term feelings of happiness are worthless; they defeat the purpose. Besides, it's easy to reach the point of exhaustion, when you no longer have the energy to put forth the effort that managing a relationship takes. A relationship is like a full-time job and is something that requires daily effort and attention. Successful, daily work gives the relationship the drive it needs to stay afloat. People will remember those things you left unaccomplished. On the other hand, they also seem to quickly forget the things you did from the heart; those things which were lovingly accomplished. In a relationship, it's the small things that count the most; people most likely will appreciate them.

Nevertheless, it's whatever we take for granted that haunts us like people coming back from the grave.

However, the mythical beauty of women alone should fascinate men. But, many men have truly lost their dignity when it comes to women. Their quest is never shallow; men live to always tread deeper waters. This is the centerpiece of some men; their focus is their search of one thing only. Nevertheless, today's women let men play themselves, because, women now know where a man's weakness lies. A woman holds the power for, her treasures are the truth of reality. Therefore, a woman can make or break a man's will and with the power of manipulation, she controls him. One example, to further explain , this statement is, if a woman stops having sexual intercourse with her man, he will suddenly reveal a face with sad puppy dog eyes. Some men will even cry or beg just to taste the scent of her breath. Furthermore, this is the level of dignity and morals that some of today's men have stooped to; only seeking immediate sexual gratification. Nonetheless, some women are subconsciously telling men "To lay down, roll over, sit and maybe I'll give you a little bit."

If some men start realizing that women aren't prime choice pieces of meat, maybe then, they'll get more out of the relationship. For, example, it's so ironic that there are more women attending colleges, and universities than men. It's sickening that men consequently think that this is an opportunity to engage in extra curriculum activities by pursuing all the women their hearts desire. With the increased number of women obtaining college degrees, women will become the leaders of tomorrow. Unfortunately, some men will always seek to conquer and experience different women. Furthermore, it's very rare that you'll find a man who's only had one woman during his life span. Some men have animalistic instincts which make them subjectively see women as prey. I respectfully state that a woman with good morals should be given her due in today's society. However, some women have become modern day jezebels and they exploit their mythical beauty.

The beauty of a woman is for the world to see, but her adornments should be for her partner's eyes only. Instead, some women get it twisted, and they like the attention that they receive from other men. This gives some women a sense of aura about themselves, as they feel the effects of their beauty. Some men notice other attributes women may pay very little attention to. Therefore, many women believe this statement and they carry themselves with dignity and respect. The best, for women, is yet to come in today's world. The trend has changed for women; the future will understand her greatness. Women have made great contributions to society and they'll continue to do more. Women will reach the point of acceptance in the work force; they'll be judged on their ability to perform and complete a task effectively.

Women want to be understood in their relationships. They also want to know that problems and issues in the relationship will be resolved. Women need to feel a sense of reassurance during their relationships.Often, that's why women make gestures or display negative body language; sometimes they feel very unsure about things. Therefore, men should make use of communicating effectively, in order to resolve any issue at hand. Secondly, men need to make sure the women feel that they are a part of the solution in resolving the issues that may arise. Then most women will open up and state their complaints or concerns. This starts the solution cycle of what many people find so problematic in today's relationships. Some people will not continuously relate. Consequently, a person's mindset plays an important role, because the mind is constantly changing. What might be understood between the parties today, could be subject to change tomorrow.

In a relationship, sometimes change is good or sometimes it is bad. However, it's true that nothing stays the same and is forever. Change should always improve a situation or circumstance. But, changes for the worst rather than the best, attribute to conflict in any relationship. The feelings of both people involved must be in agreement with the intent to carry out change. Furthermore, within the boundaries of change, communication with proper feedback is the source of change. Nonetheless, once both parties in the relationship have reached a mutual agreement, the change can be implemented. This is how change should take place in relationships, but unfortunately it doesn't happen this way. A change must bring about a form of expression or something that gives new direction. However, never try to change the real you because some people will give off vibes of approval and others will dislike you for their reasons alone. Stay true to yourself besides, you can't please everyone all of the time.

Basically, today's relationships have moved from the arena of principals, to the arena of uncertainty. It has become very difficult for each individual to be content and happy in the relationship. Indeed, at one time or another the relationship will struggle, but it must have the ability to survive. The goal or level of achievement should be to become secured in all aspects of life. Variety is the norm for many people that are in a meaningful relationship; this is socially incorrect and is considered to be wrong, but it happens redundantly. What have our ancestors and our forefathers instilled in us, for we are the products of them. One must try to grasp some form of understanding to rationally make sense of it all. The American dream has transformed and is now somewhat misunderstood; our youth are growing up in households without both parents. Many people live this way in our society, however, it goes beyond the fact of what life is all about.

People change...

Chapter 2

Control

-Without the writing on the wall

In your eyes would I stand tall

Sometimes in life we all take the fall

But your science fiction tales of me

Could easily structure or format

A book or a biblical

Why of me are you so analytical

It's degrading for you to break me down

To a simple science that is hypothetical

And somewhat political

When something is wrong to make it right

We must correct

For I am not a study, a survey,

Or a college subject

Yes, no to your way of thinking

I strongly object...

People will always seek some form of control, at one time or another in their relationships. This control is pursued for the sole notion of power which has the potential to hurt the love within any relationship. Nonetheless, love is a good thing, but control is what suffocates its passion. A successful and healthy relationship allows the parties within the relationship to breathe. Without freedom of choice and some sense of trust, internally souls will die. If someone loves you, they'll allow you freedom, with the belief that the power of love, is faith. Some people play mind games in relationships by utilizing reverse psychology. Once the weakness or soft spot is made known to the controlling partner, he or she begins to use it as a weapon. In certain situations, the controller starts to control his or her partner's behavior by often revisiting the area of weakness where the soreness dwells.

A controlling person lacks trust in others, consciously, or subconsciously. They place people in 2 categories, controllers and those who are controlled. Controllers assume that if they are not controlling their partner, then by default, their partner must be controlling them. Some partnerships have one person who dominates, while others swap the controlling position back and forth, in a chess-like game, in hopes of getting their cause heard. This group displays the healthiest form of control in a relationship, because both parties will control at some point or another. However, receiving the feeling of power and authority is paramount to all else in a relationship for the controller. This helps explain why people who manipulate often seem irrational in their reasons for controlling someone. For example, a controlling woman may ask her partner to constantly retrieve trivial items for her while at home or the man might demand that his spouse phone him constantly to update him on her whereabouts. The purpose of the task or routine itself is irrelevant. The fact is, that one person in the relationship is successfully dictating the behavior of the other person.

Control can damage the relationship when someone who is controlling makes a continuous effort to discontinue your dreams. Never submit to granting someone this much power over your mind. The mind should be a force that allows progression to be constant. Nevertheless, the goal of the controller is to prohibit his or her partner's ability to achieve. If given the chance with consent and support from their partner, some people will accomplish their goals. Specifically, it's the negative feedback from the controller that disables the partner's motivation, initiative, and desire. Some people will tell you things to stop your thought process. Don't ever listen to words of negativity; they are meant to hinder your potential, for these negative words shouldn't carry any weight. Always follow the words of encouragement because they'll be your source of persistence. Consequently, positive feedback will never make a person procrastinate; it actually permits the drive that some people need. For all the people that have had the negative type of control over your life, forgive them, and heal yourself with the power of love. Because, at some point, someone else will control the controller. It certainly holds true, that "What goes around, comes around."

With the thought of controlling someone, controllers will often set their own scenario. For instance, countless controlling situations steal segments of one's self actualization. By simply getting people to do what we want them to do, we can clearly make an argument that this is a form of motivation; however motivation is only effective when utilized in a positive sense. The problem with motivation is that it involves the interactions between people. Principally, human beings will always have flaws which can make motivation become a form of control, if one's intentions are bad. An insecure person worries about the outcome or result of any situation, simply because of his or her own fears of failure, which is in itself a weakness, and causes one to have a need to control something or someone. Being secure with one's relationship, and having freedom to proceed without fear, enables a well balanced partnership. Once the partner's basic and security needs are met adequately, in the relationship, they will both feel a sense of belonging.

But, once one confronts the controller and he or she knows that you're no longer a part of his or her evilness, the very next time the controller so happens to cross your path you'll notice the willingness of the controller to let you make choices for yourself. For example, controllers can't grasp what they can't hold; respect and understanding are the enemies of controllers because respect and understanding don't allow freedom of choice to be locked away. Control is the darkside of some people's personality, which will permit the heart to die. A relationship that enables both parties to have some form of freedom, is a healthy relationship; trust compels the relationship to be a bond solely made of love. If your partner is controlling and seemingly wants to leave or break up whenever there's some kind of disagreement in your relationship, you should put your partner's tools to work and test the durability of your relationship. Because manipulation and control are blunt tools thrust upon the fine artwork of a healthy relationship. Therefore, a canvas painted with a roller brush of manipulation and control will never become a masterpiece.

However, even if someone is fortunate enough to reach the pinnacle in life, all the social devices that people encounter to obtain this level, will make one susceptible to the realities of life. Therefore, never give someone the right to control your life. Because as the years go by, you'll realize that you never really lived . Besides, the importance of life is everyday that you're above the dirt. Be happy and live your life with vigor and strive to achieve whatever your heart desires. Your individuality and freedom will always speak volumes above people who control others. Furthermore, it's the individuality within you that let's them hear your voice. Suddenly, the controller will realize all the times that you have cried just for his or her's understanding. Secondly, freedom is what must always live within you because it gives you a chance to make choices. Sometimes the choices or decisions that you make can reward you with long awaited days in the sun. Nonetheless, the controller wants so badly to forbid this because they would prefer that you don't see the light of day.

Principally, it's shocking that we live in a society where the practice of control and deceit in a relationship attribute to many people becoming psychologically fractured. The subconscious state of mind is somewhat emotionally scared and it secures the actualization of pain. People will continuously store memories of all the times they have experienced pain. Thusly, we function in a society where many people momentarily believe in the healing power of love. For this reason only, many people are finding themselves lost in pain. However, if one factors the pain that one experiences, along with control and deceit, one will find it difficult to trust again. Because sorrow and hurt will always equal someone's pain that remains.

Yet, controllers will still look into your eyes and give you a smile that says, "I would never hurt you." Indeed, they willingly do; they know that you'll suffer in the relationship, in due time. The controller latches on to your heart for nourishment like a blood-sucking parasite, and consequently he or she feeds off your vulnerability. This type of controller means you no good and their intent is to cause you great pain. However, time is the solution to help one's recovery from the harshness of the controller. Nonetheless, if you take a moment to reflect back, you'll realize that the controller never really loved you. But, the thought of it all will make one question himself or herself, over and over again. Specifically, one must understand that control isn't unconditional love, because love will let you feel its compassion abundantly. Certainly, a relationship shouldn't warrant the need for someone to dictate his or her partner's behavior constantly.

Most controlling relationships put people on a course where there will be a need to survive. Because controllers can't feel the heartache of sorrow that one feels. Besides, they prefer to keep your heart at its darkest moment so that you continuously live among despair. Although, controllers will compromise, sometimes it's only just to suit the phase or the situation in the relationship. But, they'll still maintain a firm hand when it comes to getting their point heard. Also, they verbally make you aware of their control by insinuating your lack of consideration for the relationship. Controllers trick their partners into feelings of guiltiness all just to maintain law and order.

Some controllers rule with silence; their body language and facial expressions always will demand change. This plots the way things will be played out in the relationship. Controllers of this type, feel no love for their partners, and they'll inflict pain in order to always stay in control. Nevertheless, partners will remain dedicated, to this type of controller, because they are often given the opportunity to voice their opinions. Therefore, these partners may develop a false sense of empowerment, and a false sense of control, in their relationships. In actuality, the silent controller dictates what should be carried out, without saying a single word; the power of the controller's gestures, make his or her partner, simply recant, thusly, they speak with contradiction. Controllers use this method of control to make their partners feel as though they have control in their relationship. Principally, oriental women play the role of being very submissive, as a result, their partner feels an extreme sense of control in the relationship, but without the submissive woman's assistance, the controller becomes very reluctant in his decision making. This is because he has developed a need to be depended upon by her and his abilities to function independently have atrophied.

Controllers are equipped with the intent that badly influences life. However, people must step up to the plate with the bat in their hands and if someone takes the bat away, then they must create one of their own. Thusly, life is the chance we take but having controlling partners in our relationships will put a damper on our efforts. Nonetheless, control in many relationships can be healthy, if the nature of control is favorable to both partners. But, if someone abuses control, this type of understanding isn't healthy for any relationship. Simply, controllers have an inherent need to manipulate control, as a result of their belief that their partners wouldn't make decisions favorable to them; and controllers feel the relationship wouldn't succeed if the natural process of the relationship were permitted to take its course.

Specifically, we live for the moment that our souls consequently cry and die. Tough love has become more a part of people's lives, than true love. Sometimes, I wonder if people see the world through a different set of eyes. Nevertheless, the controller in the relationship will also, use the criteria of tough love as an effective resource. When a controller is faced with the prospect of having no one to control, he or she is forced to become introspective, if only long enough to control the next person. This gives the controller an overall self-examination, an internal look at all the pain that he or she has caused. In some cases, the controller may be unaware of his or her tendencies. However, the pain the controller causes still hurts. Most controllers are aware of their tendencies and they faithfully adapt to this type of behavior. People who are being controlled in their relationships should make a sincere effort to defeat the controller.

Look carefully into the eyes of people who control others and you'll see that their intentions are wicked. Quickly, begin to realize that controllers live on the soul of their partners, and showing or giving mutual love is senseless to them. Controllers inflict their internal sadness upon people of good intent and they'll convert them into people with fears. Indeed, controllers use their partners as fools in a game that they repeatedly play. Many controllers also have the notion that the sound of their voice has the power to hold one submissively in love. Thankfully, real love doesn't work this way, because true love will always show. Controllers obviously live in a different world and they cause deep pain within their partnerships. Controllers do want to be truly loved, though, their outlook reflects.

The Unloved...

Chapter 3

Deceit

- A snake can camouflage itself

Within its own surrounding

It will sometimes give way

And even give warning

To prevent you from making

A costly mistake

But what is more harmful

And most deadly

Is the lashing tongue

Of a human being

that pretends to be real

and is fake...

In today's relationships it's easy to hurt your partner dearly, but can you withstand or endure the same pain. When your partner is dishonest in the relationship, sometimes the wrong thing to do is the right thing to do, even if it's just for the moment. Never show favor to the partner who is dishonest in the relationship, because once you show him or her that no matter what happens in the relationship that you'll still always accept him or her back, the person's mindset becomes more deceitful. Therefore, your relationship will ride the rail of an emotional roller coaster. The dishonesty and deceit will most likely continue in the relationship. This danger sign, is certainly a mecca for pain and heartache. Even if you think it might somehow get better, it probably never will. Because the dishonest party senses weakness, and this makes him or her feel some form of control over you. This person will tell lies, while keeping a straight face, even without blinking their eyes. Consequently, knowing that you will believe the lies and give him or her your hugs and kisses. This is the confidence of deceit, but it lacks a heart; it has no remorse.

People who are dishonest and deceitful in their relationships, become shadows of darkness. Merely, there must be a little light that shines within people that have a heart. They possess all the intentions to show true love in a relationship; people sometimes know their loved ones love them sincerely, and yet, they still manage to hurt them. Sometimes in relationships one of the partners may have an inferiority complex in his or her relationship. This is a serious problem in some relationships because one partner will always be taken for granted. However, the self-esteem of the victim in the partnership will also suffer tremendously. It's the pain of deceit, that takes away your self-esteem. If you can somehow live through the tricks and trades of the untrustworthy, you will obtain a better awareness and understanding of yourself because " What doesn't kill you, only makes you stronger."

The partner that proves to be dishonest, breaking the golden rules of loyalty and trust, hides behind a shield of deceit and chaos. To unveil what lies just beneath the surface of any relationship of untruths and trickery, expose your partner for the world to see a clear reflection of him or her. With conviction, suddenly, the deceitful partner will begin to speak out against you, for the sole purpose of covering up all his or her wrong deeds. When your partner starts to take you down through the pits of hell, quickly flashback to what was the makings of love and trust, but now is the reality of life. Nevertheless, as you take this journey of sorrow and pain, you must pray and have faith. Desperately, hold on to your soul because your deceitful partner will seek it also. However, if your partner has the heart of the devil and can watch silently as you slowly die, leave this person as quickly as you can because they will laugh at your funeral.

Some people say, "The devil you do know, is better than the devil you don't know." Never subject yourself to the foolishness of any devil. The moment you realize that you're in a relationship with someone of devilish intent, re-evaluate your situation. Although, many people are holding on to whatever seems to be present, the meaning of love isn't pain, nor heartache. The feelings of love and happiness should stand the test of time and never die. Sometimes, it's the person that appears to be on your side that will persistently plot your demise. This type of person has hate in his or her heart for you; they would rather see you suffer. When you cry, the person drowns themselves in laughter because it's your pain and suffering that this person enjoys.

Also, depart from this type of person, because love was certainly never in his or her heart. One shouldn't try to understand the wickedness of deceit; the emotion of it all is too stressful for the mind. If this wickedness is given deep thought somehow you'd still desire the person that broke your heart. You may start to blame yourself for the things you never did. In the midst of your pain you will look for logic just to maybe make some sense of it all. Consequently, the wickedness of deceit can somehow still hold your heart.

Some people will tell you that they love you and never really mean it. Nevertheless, they wait for the chance to stab you in the back, and watch as your heart bleeds. They also hate the brightness of your smile or other good traits that follow.

One must obtain a better understanding of the mechanics that deceit demands. Deceit will ask one to understand and accept its sickness, also, to believe lies regardless of the pain that they cause. Deceit even wants you to endure all of its foolishness and greet it with the warmth of love. For example, many people pretend that they're in love with that special someone, however if the relationship inhabits miscommunication or disagreements, some people will elude to cheating. Nonetheless, their new partner must be able and ready at all times; this is the standard that deceitful minds will demand. In a world of cruelty, people have to find the ability to be strong and sometimes stand alone.

Untruths of deceit are always followed by demand, with a mixture of lies or fabrication of the truth; deceit prefers to stand. It will beg for your forgiveness and mercy because it wants you to accept things and just let them be. Therefore, in a world of lies the truth shall always stand. We all suffer the pain of deceit, because people have fears that scare them like the sound of boo. So, in today's relationships people experience difficulties which don't enable them to reveal friend or foe, because deceit will fool one initially. Although, we live in a world where love and trust should be the common link, within our society deceit makes its claim to fame by keeping its name in lights high above the marquee. Many people in modern relationships suffer and die at the hands of deceit.

Some people have the ability to fool you with the wickedness of deceit. The insecurities in some people, often reveal the potential for them to be deceitful. Besides, these people live among the lies that they've told you before. True love cannot identify with lies and deceit. But, deceitful minds have the nerve to expect your heart to dwell where fools do. Principally, one must make it his or her duty to be familiar with deceitful people. Look for the smile that excessively complains and expects you to be a problem solver. For, these people want so badly to make you aware of their differences because they need your acceptance to perform their deceitful deeds. Immediately, after one accepts the soul of deceit, one soon feels the receptors of pain.

Deceitfulness is nothing short of behavior with bizarre tendencies, however for many people it's the norm. Thusly, some people have given up on love and they live off of the lust of deceit. This is a painful way to live your life; it's almost like getting all dressed up with no place to go. Specifically, your heart won't feel the exhilaration that love has to offer. The fire that should burn within your soul, will never be one of happiness and joy. Therefore, many people live on the coldness of deceit and the pains of life. Because the moment you live for your belief in love, deceit will come and crush your heart in the night. So many people want love that's perfect and pure like winter's snow, but deceit will always crave the flesh of others and expect you to understand.

However, some people will always believe in the power of love, and they shouldn't take the blame for deceit's actions. Continuously keep your belief system, because it will help you through your troublesome times. If you can somehow, with no fears, confront the hurt that deceit inflicts, then you can move forward in your life. The challenge is realizing that deceit doesn't have concerns for beliefs and morals; it only wants to hurt your soul. Deceitful minds will also expect you to fatten up the frog for the snake; deceit doesn't even allow a moment of silence, or just a second to consider your pain. Specifically, deceit is more concerned with mischievous gains and has no regard for your feelings. Unawareness creates a perception that often times keeps deceit in existence; but, once truth is revealed, or made known, one will begin to see clearly all the lies that deceit kept hidden in the dark.

Deceit has no decency about itself, but periodically, it reveals bits and pieces of foresight, because deceit knows that it carries the ability to hurt you tremendously. On the other hand, it wants to keep you breathing just to continue its vindictive characteristics. The suffrage is one of pain, although you believe in the equality of fairness and truth. However, deceit has the power to make you succumb internally; one's heart can't withstand the painful ordeal of deceit. Thusly, no one wants to play the role of being the fool in a relationship. Have faith in God because he will most certainly reveal the light of truth during your relationship. Nevertheless, you will fall off at some point, or another; the ride isn't forever.

But, some people will come to you with the thought to tell the truth and still lie because deceit will not permit the truth. Deceit has no difficulty expressing itself even if the focus is solely to seemingly produce good intent. You want to believe and put your trust in someone but, some people have become concerned only with themselves. The pledge to uphold trust and goodwill doesn't matter to deceitful people. Maybe, this is the reason why people have become more conscientious in relationships. The people who have love in their hearts will hope to have a relationship that's bonded with trust and love.

Principally, the deceit of one's past, enables one to make use of past love. Some people hold on to their past with grips strong as 1000 chains. Many people fail to give someone new the benefit of the doubt. We are all attached to our past, somehow, but it's our fears that bring our past into the present. There's no beauty within deceit; love must compel us to move forward. Unfortunately, people are more than sinful, in today's society. In a world of deceit and trickery, many that once had a heart of love, have become exposed,

Spirit Breakers...

Chapter 4

Pain

-Subjectively in relationships some people play the role of

being the other person

Internally the pain judges them many times over before

they face the beholder

with a constant body temperature of normal somehow they

become colder

Some people stoop to a level a demeanor of secondary

When they truly know in their heart that they're primary

However the control of demons of the past with lustful and

sinful passion

Go in and out of their life like trendsetters going out

fashion

This person battles the thought of morally doing what is

only right

But they willingly live for the night

To live your life in hell and still somehow feel that you're

living well

For some people this is where their soul dwells...

Many people have lost everything they ever had and no matter what, they can't seem to find their way. This is what untrue love does; it slowly kills the heart. Sometimes, it's better to have your heart broken all at once, instead of having it broken several times over, and over, piece by piece along the way. The people who have had their hearts broken this way; the ones in the several times over category, are lost in the sorrow of what they thought was love. Now, they live their lives on the remorse of sadness and pain. To be in love with someone who doesn't love you, serves no useful purpose. One can't begin to fathom the pain that this type of relationship causes. Love is always primary; you must be the one and only love in someone's life, in order to receive unconditional love. If you hold on to something that is meaningless in your life, everything becomes useless. Without this person in your life, you may feel that life is worthless, but this type of relationship would have an outcome of sorrow, and no one should sentence his or her heart to a multitude of deaths.

Avoid making your life loveless; don't internally wage war against yourself; this always makes you the casualty. Some people will hurt you, because they feel no love within themselves. However, this doesn't give them the right to play on your feelings and emotions. This type of person needs to be taught a lesson, in order to develop a new found respect for love. A taste of his or her own medicine is my recommended solution which will cure this person's heart symptoms. I truly believe that love can conquer all, but sometimes it must travel the path of many different phases, to refine itself.

I feel sympathy for people who try desperately to make their relationships work. These people's lives are actual, living nightmares, and they are living in fear. No one should endure this kind of pain in life; it closes love's doors to the heart and prevents opportunity and chances for true love, or makes true love more unlikely. Many people will encourage you to move on with your life, which is the right action to take in a relationship of this type. However, the past is your connection to the future, and if the past has been painful, it's most likely that in your future relationship, you could also experience pain. Life is definitely what we make of it, and "Whatever we put into it, is what we'll get out of it." Consequently, we can't help the hand that we've been dealt, but we can play it well and achieve happiness in our lives. Truthfully, some people will always hurt the heart of someone that has already endured a life of pain.

Hurtful partners will start to admit to things that you already know and hearing those words fall from their mouths makes the truth seem golden. Knowing all the things they did to hurt you, them admitting it can't heal your heart. Don't ever give them a second chance to hurt you again, because the next times the pain will run deeper. Even, if they come back to you on their hands and knees begging, turn them away. When you see a snake in the grass, always give the snake its due. The first strike was the venomous bite of pain that they placed upon you in the relationship. Indeed, some people experience the second and third strike as if they have developed an anti-venom for the hurt of love. However, the pain that people endure is present and it will become a part of them.

Images of pain that adversely effect us, stay imprinted in our memory banks forever. Consequently, the search for true love is like the search for the Holy Grail. Some people are quietly possessive in relationships and whenever they make love, their message is conveyed crystal clear. Some people teach what is to be learned by giving sinful pleasures and sexual blessings; it's lust that will push and shove, but true love will let you feel love. As pains hurts us dearly, we try to vanish into thin air. In a world of lies and pain, valiantly, the truth still stands. But, cherish the belief in love and never say "Never will I fall in love again," besides, that's when love will find you. Thusly, the search for love is the reality of life, that somehow forgets the formality.

Perhaps the darkness of night can always be reborn. However, the fact of the matter is, that whatever is inside you will keep the lamp burning long after the kerosene is gone.

Facing truth is the true reality of life. No one can change the past in the midst of mayhem. We all have the tendency to size one another up, therefore, painful experiences will continue to holds us with guilt. During those times that we have lied down with the devil, and the beast asked for our soul, we survived because God had mercy on us and showed us his love. The Lord knows what you really endure and he understands your pain. People will scorn your name, but only God can judge you. People will never understand all the times you have given from your heart. Whenever you said here is my heart, don't hurt me, it was pain that you suffered. Some will smile as though they are happy and content, but their smile contains their pain.

Reliving, the happy moments can be used as a defense mechanism to help one cope with the pains of life. A moment in your soul can somehow last forever. If it has been preserved with internal love and care. However, pain will always destroy your happiness it comes with the same effect that can't be subdued. Besides, people feel and know the presence of pain because it wants to stay with them. As it reminds someone all the times he or she has laughed and pain wasn't present. It's the feeling in your heart that lets you know pain can hurt you so bad. Nonetheless, to be held and healed with the power of love is nothing short of a miracle. However, it's the pains of life that keep us lost in our fears. But, pain can't solely carry the blame because people rejuvenate its sorrow. That's why it hurts for people to sincerely accept things for what they truly project. But, life will always bring some form of pain just to arrive at happiness again. Because pain is a part of life that some people convert into inner strength. But, if we lived in a world of no heartache and no sorrow, pain wouldn't exist. Realize however, that valuable lessons of life couldn't be learned if pain was elusive. But, in some situations common sense is better than any knowledge that one can be taught.

Sometimes in relationships when people hurt you internally the pain wants to settles.

Specifically, the emotion of love will miraculously forgive pain and one will fall in love again. But, pain can only be forgiven not forgotten even with the power of love. Therefore, our mindset has been conditioned to feel and believe that love must hurt. Most certainly, pain can never be love . It's a form of punishment that sometimes transcends into a lingering suffrage or perseverance. However, pain has put many spirits to rest because once a person's spirit dies, the body will soon follow. Furthermore, pain will always keep love assuming the worst in any relationship. One should be thankful to have a relationship that doesn't dwell where pain and sorrow live. Thusly, pain is the poison of love that seems to gain strength with time. Therefore, people die repetitively for the sake of pain, and they embrace the arms of pain like it's a part of their soul.

The pain that people experience is similar to body tattoos because after the scabs heal the marks still remain. Sometimes tattoos reveal the story of someone's life and what they have endured. With a heart of hurt, there is no doubt that certain behavior do put people at risk for physical ailments. Due to the emotional marking of pain some people exhibit patterns of behavior with no discipline. Specifically, people display a collection of behaviors they are sometimes being impatient, easily aroused, hostile or angry. Because pain is especially profound in today's society we succumb to its sadness. Pain is the main factor why some people fail to establish close and long-term relationships.

Nevertheless, the result is loneliness and long periods of social isolation. As I observe people, I suddenly realize that many people have no spirit because the pain of their past has taken the life right out of them. Unfortunately, we live in a society where pain is present and its people are unstable. Some people live in a sedative coma-like state where nothing causes them pain.

Love and pain will always endure conflict however it's the pain that eliminates your personal power. Some people will cause you pain and never really believe that you mattered. Therefore, one can't live on the memories of sadness and pain because the present is what ultimately matters. Principally, it's all the times that you had to swallow your pride in your relationship just to keep peace in your home. It was you that cared for pain with a heart that forgives sincerely. I really understand that we live in a world where many people will come to know pain. But, I can't understand why so many people have become strangers when it come to love.

A beautiful young lady once told me that people didn't like her for some reason or another. She also stated that her external beauty was light years beyond her enemies. She boosted and bragged about all the materialistic possessions that she had obtained in her life. However, I felt the sadness that was within her and I saw the ugliness of her internally. She had lived a life of pain and all the spoils and lavish gifts couldn't ease her sadness. Some people never received the ability to love someone truly and their heart hurts for that kind of love. Their fears make them secondary and they look for what seems to be safe. But, to live your life without love is the sadness of loneliness. Always remember to never let someone see all of your weaknesses because people who know such things about you, may mistreat you purposely.

The experience of pain can really hurt your heart but the healing process is slightly redundant. For example, the way individual's hearts may hurt is similar to the way they want to be healed. Therefore, deceitful hearts will always hurt people that truly believe in love. But, a heart of love wants to heal with the hopes that it won't experience pain again. In today's society many people have become friends of misery. As a result, no one escapes the clutches of pain this disease is universal. All people can relate and feel the power of pain because it's the sorrow that makes people desire true love.

I believe that people can overcome pain. The solution is to live in the moment. People need to understand that their past experiences are tools of learning. In the here and now, we have the potential to make a difference. The second that just passed is already a part of our past. Our day to day experiences of learning are constantly being compressed. Therefore, summarized and organized by technology such as searchable databases on the internet and specialized web sites however a process of the future. The online community known as "Swarming" will allow countless persons to report to the web site. The locations and activities of persons political and social movements as they occur move and change. Our hopes to ease pain lies with the power of knowledge and technology.

But, people will always have a need for the interaction of responsive touch.

Inspite of the obstacles that people will undoubtedly encounter in the future, I believe that many people will be aided with a bolstered sense of self-important. Also, I believe that people will be considered as valuable citizens. Because they'll somehow learn to live with pain and began to show one another respect, dignity, and freedom of choice. Furthermore, I believe that people will continually strive to improve their quality of life.

In our future relationships we'll respond to one another's needs, with sensitivity to each other's culture. However, some people will still have hardened hearts and they'll seek the souls of others. Also, they'll grow to resent the people that love them unconditionally. Principally, some people will be lost in the ways of wild, and they'll continue to inflict pain upon people who have a heart of love. These people true reflection will reveal the shame of what they have become.

Candles of darkness.

Chapter 5

Life

-Sometimes things that have taken place

Can't be erased

It somewhat defeats the purpose

With no pace

Memories live encoded in our minds

Recalled scenes that only time will find

Life has meaning and love is blind

So always give your all and do your best

Because for the weary there is no rest

For life is a constant battle a test...

Life is beautiful and precious but it become worthless when we give into our fears.

Let's live life, giving ourselves a fighting chance to follow our dreams. To never leave a trace of your legacy is saddest way to live or die. Life is a vivid memory in time with moments that stay engraved in our minds forever. Although, pain has become a part of life we must still seek answers. Life is the merry go round that at one time or another everyone gets on. Recalling an old nursery school rhyme or simply a song that takes you back down memory lane is life. It reveals the magical transitional period in life that can never be relived just the way it was again. However, some people are so afraid to take a chance in life. With fear of the impossible they never plot their own course. Many people are quickly satisfied and find it much easier to follow suit. Nevertheless, distraction and fears limit talent and creativity. For example it's the self-sabotage that always keeps the undiscovered rock band hidden in the garage.

In life people will tell you the impossible will never happen. For this is the most ironic thing about life. When the naysayer's utter those words out of their mouth look into their eyes, and tell them that life has unlimited possibilities. Sometimes people will bring you news that isn't always pleasant or favorable. However, it has all the possibilities of knocking you off your feet. Take a moment, to realize that life will mainly live out its role similar to a theatrical play. Nevertheless, life is a journey that will explore different places. But, at some point your will face a folk in the road. Sometimes things don't happen the way we plan because life has uncertainties. We encounter many different crossroads during our lifespan. However, the goals and dreams that come true in your life are meant for you. There is a need to achieve the finer things in life. Sometimes our fears get the best of us. You must face your fears at the brink of adversity, or you will never accomplish your goals.

The goal in life should be the pursuit of happiness but not at any cost. Never sellout and lose your soul for worldly possessions. Collectively gather yourself and live for the joy of happiness. Because no matter what you have obtained materially, if you don't have happiness, life is miserable. Pain and sorrow will always have a profound place in the lives of people who do not experience happiness. Everything seems to be selectively permissible, some people will succeed in life and others will not succeed. There will always be a society of the people who have and those who have-not. Nonetheless, the choices that we make will effect the way our life takes form.

But, sometimes during the experience of life you meet a person that is the light. They change everything bad about you into good as they bring you the faith that you never had. For this only happens once in a lifetime. It's your one wish that is granted by God. Surely, there are and will always be servants of God likewise, there will also be servants of the devil. Life should be joyful and peaceful as one endures those years. However, it's backbiting of one another the abundantly hurts us all. Some people will come just to rob you of your joy. They try to make your light dim with smiles of hatred and their venomous words that fall from their mouths.

In a world of confusion the love and respect that we as people have for one another is all that matters. Therefore, to show respect is an important attribute that people should always have for one another. Respect is the needed ingredient that always gets a friendly result. Yet, people have the right to make choices and truly they do not have to respond to your demands. Consequently, the people that are most likely to be successful in life have no problem showing respect. However, one must be aware of people that are over zealous because there is a deeper hidden agenda. Somehow you suddenly begin to be more careful, since life brings about insecurities. It's our fears that make us all momentarily deranged. Specifically, some people stay in this phase longer than others do. There is a missing void that people have when they spend the majority of their time being too careful. In the process of trying not to make mistakes along their way.

People will make mistakes because that's just life's plan. I strongly believe that human beings have the right to be protective. On the other hand, there's room in the world to have a little fun because people need leisure time also.

Furthermore, people shouldn't live their lives as if they're condemned to die. Livelihood should be present with the thought that people must and can achieve. Never cheat yourself out of life because the cemetery will always be a given. One must have a definite purpose in life and persevering shouldn't be foreign to people that have struggled. Nevertheless, it's so sad that many people are afraid to live their lives. Some people live in a dream like state of mind where their world is a distance away from true reality. A world where false fears are believed to really exist. People must live their life's without fear to obtain happiness. One should feel their surrounding and breathe from their environment. As human beings we belong and we matter in life. Therefore, it's all right to live your life with the belief that faith will sustain you.

If people could find the humor and let life be the laughter. Hopefully, people will begin to grasp the true meaning of what life is all about. Nonetheless, life is what one has the will to do with a persistent effort put forth. Throughout, the years you must set the standard for life despite being judged by your peers. We are in a world of sadness and the mindset of some people seems to be lost. The words love, us, and we are powerful and enable our unity. Many times you will appear to be very misunderstood, but you must go forth with a cause in life. Because the only thing that really matters is the positive differences that you make in the lives of others.

Life can bounce you around with the power of a stormy sea. Consequently, it doesn't have to pre-warn you or give an explanation for why unexpected things happen. However, life will bring a new day and the unpredictable can happen again. But one must hold on to the lessons learned during the process of pain. Because really nothing comes with a warranty or guarantee. People are full of uncertainty, believe that tomorrow isn't promised to us. In an instant your life could be changed forever; you must hold dearly to your ability to cherish moments! People should make an effort to tell someone "I love you."   Even if, your own family experiences differences that bring about chaos within your family circle. The potential to reunite is always present because blood is thicker than water. Thusly, some people will wait patiently for your down spiral. So, in life try to stay close to your family, they are the people that will be most likely to take care of you in the future.

The most important thing about life is still the family structure. A family must spend quality time together because this time becomes special memories. These memories will enable you to remember past events that took place in your life. Yet, life is sweet but short, therefore love your family and always show love and respect. The family is your principal means of survival and you will always share a need to connect. With the power of prayer all blessings will come from God and this is what the family dream should be. Nonetheless, as we move forward in the new millennium many people will come forth and make great contributions that significantly change and improve the standard of life. Be alive...

Chapter 6

Love

-Love is the moment your heart

Nervously beats

Its hate that love defeats

Its the passion that is never lust

Its the one thing we all need

It controls us

It's what people say is blind

It's the dream of what we all

Hope we will truly find

Its the feeling we cherish

Its what we want to perish

Its the cure of pain and heartache

Its the risk we will always take

Its the sharing of hers and his

For love is what it is...

The first time your soul mate looks into your eyes, is the moment that your whole world changes. It's similar to your first kiss, that feeling that's nothing short of magical. But, the moment you experience untrue love, it's love that must find you again. However, the endurance of untrue love is pain, which will make one give off a false perception of love. Nevertheless, everyone needs to be loved; it's rare that you will find a person who doesn't need or want love. We all have the desire and need to be loved, but sometimes we fear love because we die emotionally at the hands of love's dismay, therefore we succumb to the fear of love. Consequently, hearts hurt, just to heal themselves internally, so that we give sorrow the hope for happiness.

Give love the chance that you never had and with your hopefulness and open heart, you can find someone who will genuinely give love to you. Indeed, love can be something special for you and your someone to share. However, ask yourself about the concerns and fears regarding love; be honest about love. What is the true meaning of love, and are people foreign to love's passion? Many people really do not know what it is to love someone. Often, some people will become disillusioned with the emotional stress that love brings. Love is the ultimate feeling of passion that your heart must experience, at least once in your lifetime. Furthermore, love should last a lifetime. Love is a world of compassion, and if people could overcome their differences in relationships, love would stand alone, as it grows stronger with time.

I understand that one must have aspirations and dreams of happiness in order to experience true love. If you have been fortunate enough to experience true love in your lifetime, hold on to the memories forever; they belong to you; cherish them with all your heart. If you have felt the hurt of false love, it's an emotional rise and fall that hurts, and there is no greater pain. Love makes you feel as if your heart and soul are a part of that special someone in your life. When both people feel the same degree of love for one another, they become as one. Nonetheless, people will interpret a gesture or the words "I love you" as unconditional love, however, many have lost their soul for the lack of the four-letter word.

Maybe, some people will treat you with respect, however love doesn't permit someone to take advantage of another. One must have the ability to show real love without reason, to give unconditional love just because love is within his or her heart. Many people will think of ways to escape the responsibility of showing the same affection that is given to them. In this type of relationship, the degree of love that is illustrated between both parties is one-sided. An example of this problem is one person in the relationship showing love unconditionally and the other person failing to display love regularly. However, moving to fast will not keep one intrigued about the power of love. When dealing with love, every moment, should be like the last. People should show and give love from their hearts. Because love shouldn't owe us time after time, but this is what we expect love to do.

Specifically, love shouldn't be the reason one cries tears of sorrow. Relationships should be pleasant and should embody prosperity and longevity. However, the spices of life, place good intent under the knife; love has to be true to enable dreams to come true. One should always have the heart to feel and believe that love can happen in his or her life. Even though relationships have become somewhat strange, people still need to find true love to ease the pain of sorrow. Principally, people who love you for richer and for poorer, and truly adore you and only you, is rare to find nowadays. In today's relationships, people experience the making of mass confusion and massive variety has become the norm; they rarely live out the true happiness of life.

Although, love will come with the power of separation, meaning it can be good or it can be bad, depending on who you were with, one should want and desire love that will make the soul pure again. Because we all need love and understandably our hearts want to be content. Without love, we miss out on the paradise, but especially the power of love has been somewhat abused. Some people are still dimming the lights in the bedroom, though nothing is taking place that is special. Emotionally, some people live and die daily just so they can feel as if they are loved. Love is similar to a beautiful song that flows like a rushing river. Nevertheless, if the other person isn't feeling emotions that are somewhat the same as yours, you are not experiencing true love. Love will reveal itself, showing on a consistent basis. In this world where most people are searching for their own identity, we have somehow lost touch. Many people want to be recognized as real or different, but people must find something in common with one another. As people reflect back on their lives, indeed they will realize some of the things they did were good and some were bad, but it is ultimately love that kept them safe. When you were down and out, it was someone loving who came along and helped you find your way.

These loving people should be considered as guides who keep you warm through the storm. Although, in your time of need your friends may turn against you, try to show no malice. Sometimes you give with no compensation and suddenly you realize that you barely survived; perhaps life is the pain itself. We all are no different and even with hearts that want to give, we sometimes stumble, because we are not made of perfection. Love has at times, lost its luster but still needs to shine brightly. Love should still hold honor, despite the chaotic world we live in. Relationships have moved far beyond the rim of love, trust, and loyalty; some insincere people will look into your eyes and tell you they love you, just for the sole purpose of saying the words. However, the power of love is still strong enough for you to cherish. The complexity of love prohibits you from understanding all its possibilities, yet everything has meaning.

If you're alone and feel that you have arrived at your darkest moment, many nights you may toss and turn or cry yourself to sleep. Nevertheless, your peace of mind will resurface around the fact that you no longer have to live a lie. However, if someone says I love you, he or she should truly mean it, for the heart is fragile but some people play with it as though it's made of stone. If you can find inner strength to never give up on love, then as time goes by love will find you. Hold on to your belief in love, for it's the light to truth, which should reside within you. Don't base your life around lustful pleasures because after the sweat dries, your heart will still crave true love. Furthermore, your feelings will get the best of you in due time; a lustful way of life will only bring you heartache and pain. True love is often forgotten but it's the one thing we all need.

Give Love...

Chapter 7

Humanity

-For the world is sometimes a funny place

But it's not all smile

People sometimes self-destruct just to confirm

that the impairment is still there

However the lack of light will always bring darkness

People die repetitively from their own despair

Because somehow self-hatred has forbidden

unconditional love...

It's puzzling that so many people don't even believe in their own dreams. Our culture should encourage values to strive for excellence. The innovated balance between our personal and professional lives lie in the arena of the abnormal. It seems to me that society is just living to party. The night life has become our leadership. We as citizens should make a commitment to practice efficient ethical values. To build a healthy and safe environment to enable successful relationships, we must uphold trust and goodwill for one another. Today our society has embraced the lowest standards of morals. The vices that attribute to racial behavior have created a no merit, no integrity, free enterprise for chaos. My hope is that we as people find ourselves. We are the lost children, that compete for superiority. Distrust and deceit is our outlook, with this mindset, there is no room for knowledgeable growth. It's sad to say but we basically live in a world where anything is possible. Something is missing the answer is hidden. All people have an individual responsibility to serve mankind. Although, many people have made great contributions to society and they're considered as humanitarians. Our entire nation in fact lacks the basics of knowing the importance of what really matter to us. We as people have failed to protect our families, our children, our elderly and ourselves. As I observe what is presently taking place in the world today, it appears to me that people sometimes feel that nothing really matters. Furthermore, the things that people should always ensure the safety of seem to be unsafe. We lack safety nets for our health concerns, home environment, and workplace; all of those things have become society's danger zones. Somehow things have taken a turn for the worst; nothing is quite clear.

The world is based on a faulty foundation. A continuous struggle is needed to form meaningful relationships that will last a lifetime, this is unfortunate. Nowadays, people feelings for one another have begun to change quicker than the weather. Today's relationships do not provide a true connection between both parties. Maybe some of the social factors that were stated earlier, attribute to this problem.

Once again, I state to you that something is missing. The challenge to all people should be accountability. What can you as a human being account for in life? What have you given to mankind with conviction and purpose? Who has the heart to give with love and share wisdom and wealth? Nevertheless, it is easy to hold on to all the things one may have accomplished during a lifetime. This is the challenge that we face in the world today. Meanwhile, the world waits for no one and we're only here for a short stay. In a positive sense make a difference; do all that you can do. Don't live the life of the living dead while you're here on this earth. Everyone has a calling in life, quickly find out what you do best and make it manifest.

We live in a world were sex and drugs have become the roots of the world's evilness. The standard of some men has drop tremendously because they have fallen victim to this trap. Some men throw themselves at the feet of these vices. However, these vices tighten the headband intellectually for some men. Therefore, some men may not be able to think rationally. Somehow, we have suddenly reached the point that dooms us for failure. We as people need to feel a sense of inner peace. The serenity of knowing that you're totally balanced within yourself, is your sense of well being. Instead, some people are controlled by these vices and they let them dictate their behavior in relationships. Many people have no regard for the loved ones that they may have at home. Curiosity and lust controls their thought pattern in relationships with these people. This type of promiscuous behavior comes about when someone repetitively gives himself or herself to people who do not love them. Nevertheless, many people live on the souls of other partners. To live your life like this will never bring you happiness. Indeed, for a relationship to workout, it must have some spiritual substance. One must believe or stand for something or he or she will fall for anything. Find a partner that somehow still believes in love and one that has made peace with God.

We cry at the brink of pain or despair however the lesson has never been absorbed by society. I believe with all of my heart that society will find its soul. Because we have exhausted all the other avenues and still haven't resolved our problems. Although, no one knows the moment, the minute, the hour, that death can become a part of our life, we displace death and think that we'll live forever. For, it's God that is the creator of us and we will never be able to blow the breath of life. But, the true sadness is that society lives on the strength of ignorance. It seems that we are searching for the cause for us to unite. Thusly, the answer lies with the power of love. We should give one another love without the slightest of doubt. However, it's the anticipation of self-destruction and tragedy that ridiculously brings some people closer to one another.

Men and women must be able to coexist in today's society. This will enable continuous progress and growth in the world that we live in. Regardless of the complexity of today's relationships, both persons must find the median point to deal with the problems of the world today. The world is a place that needs citizens to function on a productive level.

We are the people of this nation and it's our duty to be role models and humanitarians. In the near future technology will become more advanced, more than we could ever imagine. Specifically, we must keep pace with the world of tomorrow. Furthermore, the youth of today will carry on this legacy which will plot the course of our future. Many people are dying all too soon, at the expense of someone else's hands. I certainly understand that people will live and die but I can't understand taking someone's life for no reason at all. We must realize that life is the gift that has so much value.

So many people have lost respect for themselves, which is the source of the problem. To carry yourself with respect and dignity should be the loyalty that people uphold for themselves. Nevertheless, in today's society, to reach some people you have to lie down in the gutter with them. However, to trust them fully is something you probably wouldn't want to do. Because if people can't respect themselves, how can they respect others.

Ultimately, someone must deal with the issues that these people have encountered. For they shouldn't be observed as a lost cause, although the odds are against them. We all have our faults and in life everyone is so quick to become judge and jury. People can change for the better at any given time in their life, even if we are all doomed to experience pain. Life is still so precious and it will always have value and meaning.

Furthermore, life will always test us to see if we have the uncanny ability to persevere. Sometimes in life things will seem to appear a little fuzzy instead of visibly clear. It may feel as if your whole world has begun to crumble, quickly, collectively gather yourself and roll with the punches and tumble. But, at the same time you must find the inner strength to remain humble.

However, it's unfortunate that our minority youth's historical knowledge is relegated only to familiarization of

Martin Luther King and Jesse Jackson. Our educators, across the nation, have failed to properly educate our minority youth's awareness of people that have made a difference before their time is of importance. Because the human experience is a continuum for the wise, but for the unwise life is a process of starting over. For example, "Fools rush in where angels fear to tread" that's why people constantly make mistakes in their lives. Nevertheless, in today's society the youth must measure up even if fear unbalances the scales. They have a responsibility to make a difference and change life for the better by plotting the course of this nation.

We are in a constitutional crisis, and we all have questions and concerns. As our nation's youth feel alienated form their family, and they look to the streets for love. Principally the youth also depend on the power and influence that hip-hop music has in the world today. Perhaps, someday we will confront the alarming threats to our youth in today's society. However, one can clearly argue that we live in a world of triumphs and tragedies. Nevertheless, this argument doesn't give us the right to stay "Why bother"

The brutal outburst of racial hatred in society today call for people to examine themselves. We are living in a hostile world, facing threats to our mental and physical well being. Most people fear for their very own safety on a daily basis. Our communities across the nation have become killing fields. Also our youth are full of anger and rage because we have failed to give them their true identity. Furthermore, our youth are lost in the sadness of world's sorrow. We live in an age of falling standard, however the present-day betrayal of trust in our personal lives is our worst enemy. Often, people are becoming lovers of themselves with no need for natural affection. Consequently, this the outlook of many people in today's society. The decline of moral standards goes hand and hand with the problems of the world. Despite the world's distress and the hurt of its people, love is the answer.

However, the population of people incarcerated will increase in alarming numbers. Also, to ensure the equality of freedom and equal opportunity in life, people will seek the need to exercise their rights more often. We do not realize that the hunt is on for our freedom and collectively as people the love is not in our hearts for us to come together. Some people are just living for today, with no hope or thought of what the future will bring.

Nevertheless, the inhumane treatment of the people who were treated like cattle and slaughtered because of texture of their skin, by far, was the worst crime in history committed against mankind. Slavery was the historical tragedy that forever cursed us as people. The instilled conditioning of hatred that over 440 years of oppression brought about is a suffrage of evil that is now called violence today. Furthermore, the same hatred has been passed down from one generation to the next and socially as people we're lost in a cabal of wickedness. Therefore, the body count will continue because historically this world has always bred violence.

There is a growing need for culture diversity in this world. It's important to learn and experience different characteristics about other people. One must know or have experienced something about the culture of a person that has a different nationality. People can have long-term relationships with a person that they must learn more about, to understand. Racially this nation has suffered throughout history and still there is racial discrimination today. I feel that culture diversity can bridge the racial gap that deeply damages the people of this nation; its obvious our wombs have not completely healed.

People are most likely to form favorable relationships with someone that has similar interests. However, I believe that a diverse nation of people will enable different ethnic groups to make the connection and overcome the racial gap that divides us as people. If we as people are willing to breakdown the racial barriers that have exhausted the nation's minds, perhaps then we can begin to understand the true meaning of what humanity is all about.

However, it may seem I truly believe that people can mend and iron out their differences. In the future, I really believe that people will need one another more than ever. Meanwhile, the population of our elderly may double in the near future. An enormous amount of helping hands will be much needed to take care of our elderly. We owe this to them for they are the builders of our nation. To demonstrate helpful humanity, is the right thing to do in this matter. We as people must begin to show concern and consideration for one another. The years of change have somehow taken the trust away. Indeed, people are still living in fear of this or that. I still believe that some people are meant to be together regardless of the perplexity of today's relationships. People should try to form relationships and friendships that are based on trust and not deceit. Sincerely, it's my hope that we all can live in perfect harmony. We are a social bunch that will always have a need to seek one another. The potential for greatness and glorification is the standard of excellence, but what lies beneath the surface is always the potential for self-destruction.

Nevertheless, a warm smile and a pleasant demeanor can also be a false perception. Consequently, behavior is and will always be unpredictable. Therefore, the potential for violence is always present and can happen randomly or unexpected. Psychologically, human beings take themselves to the limit repetitively, because there is a need to constantly reform. The mind is constantly changing and under certain stresses or adverse circumstance. The probability of what will happen on a consistent basis is highly unknown. We sometimes get caught up in this fast paced world and we take life for granted. We never know how long we have to live on this earth. So, every moment that God gives us life, we must savor the moment and cherish it dearly. To show traits of loving humanity is the greatest deed that one can do. As we give ourselves in relationships many social factors come into play. They project feedback of positive reinforces or negative reinforces in a relationship which sometimes eludes to the inevitable the 3 d's which are divorce, desertion, and death. Specifically, my analysis of relationships is that we all are human with unpredictable tendencies of behavior. We all have fallen short of the requirements to have healthy and successful relationships during this process.

We falter...

Through the contents of this book I also heal.

For at times I have succumbed to the pain.

That I have endured in my own life. But somehow

I found the strength to persevere. I gave the

love that was always within me...

www.ingramcontent.com/pod-product-compliance
Lightning Source LLC
Chambersburg PA
CBHW030343290526
45785CB00004B/1579

* 9 7 8 1 4 1 8 4 7 6 3 5 9 *